I0004616

Table of Contents

Routers and setting them up

There are many brands of routers. Here are a few of the top selling routers and how to set them up for wireless use. You can find screen-shots at WWW.chasms.com. They will show you step by step for setting the router up.

Linksys:

- This router is a product of Cisco.

- Set-up for this router is easy, Cisco gives you a instalation disk that sets the router up for you.

- There may be times when you need to log into the router. To log into this router open your web browser.

- Once your browser is open look at the top of the browser and were you see HTTP:// you are going to need to clear it out.

- Once you clear that bar you will need to type 192.168.1.1. This will open up your Router page. If you did not get that page make sure you are connected hardwired not by wireless.

- This page should ask you for a username and password. There is no default username for Linksys so leave that blank. The password will be **admin**.

- In this page you can set up your router, also look at your

wireless settings always be
sure to set up a pass phrase to
secure your network. Also be
sure that the box is checked to
Broadcast your SSID. If this is
not checked you will not be
able to find your network.

Netgear

- This router is a product of
  Netgear.
- Set-up for this router is easy,
  Netgear gives you a instalation

disk that sets the router up for you.

- There may be times when you need to log into the router. To log into this router open your web browser.

- Once your browser is open look at the top of the browser and were you see HTTP:// you are going to need to clear it out.

- Once you clear that bar you will need to type 192.168.0.1. This will open up your Router page. If you did not get that page make sure you are connected hardwired not by wireless.

- This page should ask you for a username and password. The username for Netgear is **admin** and password is **password.**

- In this page you can set up your router, also look at your wireless settings always be sure to set up a pass phrase to secure your network. Also be sure that the box is checked to

Broadcast your SSID. If this is not checked you will not be able to find your network.

Belkin

- This router is a product of Belkin.

- Set-up for this router is easy, Belkin gives you a instalation disk that sets the router up for you.

- There may be times when you need to log into the router. To

log into this router open your
web browser.

- Once your browser is open
  look at the top of the browser
  and were you see HTTP:// you
  are going to need to clear it
  out.

- Once you clear that bar you
  will need to type
  192.168.2.1. This will open up
  your Router page. If you did
  not get that page make sure
  you are connected hardwired
  not by wireless.

- This page should ask you for a username and password. The default username for Belkin is **admin**. There is no password for Belkin.

- In this page you can set up your router, also look at your wireless settings always be sure to set up a pass phrase to secure your network. Also be sure that the box is checked to Broadcast your SSID. If this is not checked you will not be able to find your network.

DLink

- This router is a product of DLinkk.

- Set-up for this router is easy, DLink gives you a instalation disk that sets the router up for you.

- There may be times when you need to log into the router. To log into this router open your web browser.

- Once your browser is open look at the top of the browser and were you see HTTP:// you are going to need to clear it out.

- Once you clear that bar you will need to type 192.168.0.1. This will open up your Router page. If you did not get that page make sure you are connected hardwired not by wireless.

- This page should ask you for a username and password. There is no default username for DLink so leave that blank. There is no password for DLink.

- In this page you can set up your router, also look at your wireless settings always be sure to set up a pass phrase to secure your network. Also be sure that the box is checked to Broadcast your SSID. If this is not checked you will not be able to find your network.

Connecting to the Wireless Network

To connect to your wireless network
what you will need to do is look down
at the bottom right corner of your
screen. There should be the clock and a
couple little monitor looking things. the

wireless monitor could look like two monitors or even a monitor with waves coming out of it. Once you have located it you would need to right click that little wireless monitor and tell it to look for wireless networks in range. Once you find your network you would then connect to it and enter your wireless security key you made up when setting up your router.

Slow speed Troubleshooting

We all hate when our Internet is slow.
Before we get in to some
troubleshooting steps I must tell you
there may be nothing wrong with your

connection. With most Internet connections they are shared networks. That means that when others are using there Internet the speeds will slow down. Here are a few steps to help you be sure that everything is working properly.

Deleting Cookies/ Catch

- You will need to open your Internet Browser that you use.

- Once that is open you will need to go to options. This is usually locating in the tools menu.

- I will give you an example using Internet Exploer. When you open the Internet options it brings up a window. You will need to look about half way down the page were it says Browsing history and gives you the option to Delete. We will click on the Delete button.

- If it brings up a window giving you the option to check stuff, check the

History, Cookies, Catch then press
ok or Delete to remove this stuff.

- Now close out of your Browser

  then re-open

Disable 3rd party Extensions

- With your Browser being open lets

  go into the Internet options.

- We are looking for the advanced

  Tab at the top. Click that.

- Once you get into Advanced you

  will scroll down not far looking for

  the box that is checked that says

  Enable 3rd Party Extensions.

Once that is located un-check the box and press Apply then OK and close your Browser.

Power Cycling your Equipment

Warning: If you are using a satellite Internet Connection DO NOT UN-PLUG from behind the Modem unplug it from its power source. Examples of a power source are the wall or a power strip. Reason for this is because you can Short out your Modem un-plugging it from behind the modem.

- To begin the Power Cycle you will start out un-plugging the power to the Modem from its power source. Note some ISP's modems are also your router.

- If you have a separate router you would un-Plug that second.

- Lastly we would shut down the computer. We would wait for about a Minute then we would start by Plugging back in the Modem.

- Once your Modem is back on then plug back in the Router if you had one.

- Lastly turn back on the computer.

Run a Virus Scan

- Also a cause for slow connection is a Virus. Open your Virus Software and tell it to Run a Full System Scan.

- If you do not have Virus Protection and can get to a computer with Internet an good free virus protection is Malwarebytes. WWW.malwarebytes.org download that.

No Connection Troubleshooting

We all get mad when our Internet goes out. Here is a troubleshooting step that is the most cause for no Internet connection. If this step does not solve your issue try bypassing the Router if you have one. If that still does not work Call your (ISP) Internet Service Provider Technical Support.

Power Cycling your Equipment

Warning: If you are using a satellite Internet Connection DO NOT UN-PLUG from behind the Modem unplug it from its power source. Examples of a power source are the wall or a power

strip. Reason for this is because you

can Short out your Modem un-

plugging it from behind the modem.

- To begin the Power Cycle you will
  start out un-plugging the power to
  the Modem from its power source.
  Note some ISP's modems are also
  your router.

- If you have a separate router you
  would un-Plug that second.

- Lastly we would shut down the
  computer. We would wait for about

a Minute then we would start by Plugging back in the Modem.

- Once your Modem is back on then plug back in the Router if you had one.

- Lastly turn back on the computer.

IPconfig

- once your computer comes back on and if you still can not connect we are going to run an IPconfig.

- To run this we must first open the Command Prompt.

- Go to your Start Menu if your using windows XP click run. If using windows Vista or 7 click on that search bar and type CMD. If your using Windows 8 if your at your desktop go down to were the start menu is and Right Click and pick the option for Command Prompt with Administrative privileges. If your in your start menu screen just start typing CMD and click on the Command Prompt.
- Once you get the Command Prompt open type IPCONFIG.

- This should bring up a bunch of stuff.what we are looking for is the IP Address and the Default Gateway.

- In the newer versions of Windows you will have to get them from the IPV4 not the IPV6.

- Once you have them numbers document them for when you call Technical support . Just give them numbers to the Technition and he will know what they mean.

www.ingramcontent.com/pod-product-compliance
Lightning Source LLC
Chambersburg PA
CBHW060937050326
40689CB00013B/3131